Aspects
of
Enlightenment

Aspects
of
Enlightenment

Janet Driscoll
ADL–BSYC-MASC-PSH

THE CHOIR PRESS

First published in the United Kingdom in 2018 by
The Choir Press

ISBN 978-1-911589-95-2

Acknowledgements

With the greatest degree of love and thanks
To all my Spiritual helpers and teachers in Spirit World,
and friends who pushed me to get this book into print

Special love and thanks to my late husband
John Philip Driscoll who always encourage and supported
me to be the best I could be on my spiritual journey.

Reverend Janet Driscoll

A.D.L. B.S.Y.C. M.A.S.C. P.S.H.

International Medium and Healer

Janet was born 15 May 1944 in York, Yorkshire, England and has been mediumistic from been a child.

In 1974 a move to Devon England changed Janet's life when she became involved with the local Spiritualist Centre, and started to develop her Healing and Mediumistic gifts properly. This led to running mediumship development and healing groups, at the Newton Abbot Church Centre, and then in 1981 The Light Colour Centre at home.

Janet has been giving demonstrations of mediumship to the general public proving life after death, workshops, and Sunday Services in Spiritual Centres in England and abroad. Through recommendations, and a rare gift, she is able to work with a variety of translators.

Janet has worked at Spiritual Centres, on the continent especially in Basel Switzerland, and was the first Spiritualist medium to give a Sunday Service on the Algarve in Portugal. Janet has worked in Jersey, Holland, Spiritualist Churches, and her work has taken her to Centres in Atlanta, North Carolina, Gainesville and Florida U.S.A.

Janet gave a demonstration proving life after death. On South West Television, England. The programme was called the (Mysterious West), and was filmed at Teignmouth Spiritualist Church in Devon.

In 1998 Janet challenged James Randi the world's biggest psychic sceptic and had an article in the Psychic News.

On several occasions Janet has been asked to investigate houses, cottages, castles, act, to see if there are any ghost or poltergeist activities. If there are any earth bound spirits Janet sends them to the light.

Due to working in the USA a lot of the time in 1998 Janet became an Ordained Minister of the Alliance of Divine Love Ministry USA.

September 19th 2004 Janet was interviewed on BBC Radio Devon on Good Morning Devon in a debate on Mediumship & Spiritualism and Christianity.

Janet is a Spiritualist Medium, Ordained Minister, Spiritualist Healer and Trainer, Colour Therapist, Reiki & Seichem Master, Professional Stress Consultant, and Spiritualist Teacher and Author.

Contents

Poems created 1978–1981   1

Spiritual Teachers   2
A Bowl Of Rice   3
The Key   4
Enlightenment   6
We Are Spirit   7
The Spirit World   8
Elisabeth   10
Healing   11
God   12
God Is The Power   13
A Facet Of God   14
A Rare Seed   16
Birthday   17
A String Of Pearls   17
Children Of The Earth   18
A Facet Of Love   20
A Little Piece Of Heaven   21
No Winners   22
Humanity   23
Giving   24
Mykonos   24
Our Thoughts   25
The Gifts Of Christmas   26
Software   28
The Tree   29

The Mind   30
We Can't Take A Penny To The Sphere Above   32
Sun And Moon   33
It Always Comes To Those That Wait   34
Life Is Like A Blackboard   34
Dreams   35
Old Tom   36
Seek And Find   37
Spiritual Eyes   37
We Are All Actors   38
Listen And Advise   38
You Are Never Too Old   39
Love   40
Not For Sale   41
Heaven And Hell   42
Stress   43
The Stone   44
Freedom   45
It's Raining   46
Lonely Sea   47
Problems   48
The Crystal   49
The World   50
We Are Human Beings   52
Pride   53
Take A Risk   53
Marriage   54
Wealth   55
Worry   56
Crossroads   57
Responsibility   58
The Lamp Factory   59

Zombies   60
Moving House   61
Holland   62
Over The Air   63
You Are Never Alone   64
To Have You Here   65
Welcome Home   66

Poems created 1986   67

My Daughters   68
Children   68
A Mothers Love   69
My Mum   70
Thank You Dear Father   71

Poem created 1997   73

The Spirit Of The Universe   74

Poems created 2009   83

John Philip Driscoll   84
My Brave Husband   85
A Passing   86
Mountain   86
How Can I Live?   87
Miss You, Miss You   88
The Merry Go Round   89
Silence   90
Our House   91

We Miss You   92
Mirrors   93
Do You Love Me   94
Different Worlds   94
Is This Love   95
Heaven Sent   96
My Wonderful Husband John   97
Live, Live, Live   98
Without You   99
My Life   100

Poems created between 1978–1981

Spiritual Teachers

Everyone has Spiritual teachers they may not see
There are different teachers for every field
I have a Chinaman from a sphere above
He brings me knowledge and his love

Ching Sang Soo is his name
He was a Catholic Priest on the earth plane
He gives me poems and philosophy
Yet has never impinged Christianity on me

When I was meditating silently
I heard Ching's voice speak quietly
It came in thought needlessly
My spiritual teacher testing me

The thought came quick, I wasn't prepared
Then it was repeated word for word
It was all in rhyme and easy to remember
Spelling was a different matter

All the words I write down
Then all I do is juggle them around
I piece the words together one by one
Then to my surprise I have a poem

Most times I get a poem in minutes
I don't think, just write down the lyrics
Thank you Ching very much indeed
For all the wisdom you have taught me

A Bowl Of Rice

I handed you a bowl of rice
Without sugar, without spice
Then stood back with tears in my eyes
As you experienced tribulations and highs
If you were hungry you would eat the rice
Even though it didn't taste very nice
Planted in paddy fields underwater
Trust is put in Mother Nature

Rice is a cultivated river grass
Each grain graded then purified
Cut down sifted and sorted
Only the best grains are packed and exported
The bowl is made of china clay
It has every colour in its display
The pattern has been intricately woven
So you are ruled by your head and not emotion

Ivory chop sticks are your master
Blending the material and spiritual together
Chop sticks are difficult to use
Many grains of rice will slip though
Yet each grain caught will make you wise
Have a different story, and a different surprise
So eat what I give you it is wisdom and truth
The bowl is refilled with spiritual food

The Key

Listen new sensitive, listen to me
Ching brings to you a special key
It will open and close your psychic mind
So knowledge and wisdom can be profound
The key must be handled carefully
So keep your feet on the ground very firmly
Mediumship is knowledge and life
We can only use what is in your mind

Every gift belongs to God, not you
And can be taken away if abused
An open mind should be adopted
Any prejudice should be avoided
Not every spirit comes in love
Mischievous spirits like a look
Don't trust a spirit who claims to be
A famous person, or well-known personality

Be careful where arrogance is felt
Like attracts like so look to yourself
Not every spirit is highly evolved
Just like you we have our faults
Be patent let a spirit impinge upon you
It will leave no doubt only truth
Seek evidence and identity
Remember truth attracts sincerity

Our messages are given in love and truth
It's up to you to sift out the truth
Every contact made is an experiment
To try and prove life is infinite
We come to teach and advise
Certainly not to run anyone's life
Our work is volunteered in love
So everyone becomes a messenger for God

Enlightenment

To be enlightened spiritually
You must trust the unseen completely
There is no in-between
Meditation is the key

Enfoldment comes gradually
There is no race to spirituality
You have to earn the privilege
By life and spiritual knowledge

Spiritual teachers can then oversee
Give thoughts, feelings, and pictures to see
So you can give comfort, healing, and love
To troubled souls for the planets good

We Are Spirit

Some people don't believe in life after death
That we come to earth to go through tests
We all had a choice to be rich or poor
As most of us have been on earth before

We all have two bodies that are separate
One is physical the other is spiritual
Nothing can destroy our spiritual body
It is our self, mind, our personality

Joined by a cord to the physical body
The spirit needs experience and maturity
This is the reason theirs good and bad
So we learn from life what we can

When we die the cord is broken
We go back to where we came from
We join our loved ones on spheres above
Where time is endless and full of love

The Spirit World

It does not matter if you are rich or poor
There is no death, just a new tomorrow
The spirit world awaits us all
Everyone goes there large and small

It's just like going to another country
Full of warmth and security
You will go to a level you have earned
By the spiritual lessons you have learnt

There are no religions in the spirit world
Just large sanctuaries made of mother of pearl
Huge stained glass windows send colourful light
People go to pray, and give thanks for their life

You can learn philosophy from different minds
Listen to all kinds of music from all time
There are different sounds and emotions to feel
A wonderful experience that is surreal

There are healing hospitals in rainbow colours
Flowers, meadows, trees, and rivers
Mountains, animals, fish and sea
Better than the earth with spectacular scenes

You retain your spirit body and your mind
Material things you leave behind
But all you hold dear will be in replica
It's a Zion of infinite rapture

There is no more suffering no more pain
All your worries are left on the earth plane
Friends and loved ones you will meet
What a marvellous reunion that will be

It's a world you keep on growing
Following the interests you like doing
But most of all it's a world of love
I would take you for a look, if I could

Elisabeth

I had a vision spiritually seen
A young girl built up in front of me
She had the most beautiful face I have ever seen
Happily smiling and full of glee

Fair hair on her shoulders, like an angel serene
Passed with consumption aged thirteen
Victorian clothes she was dressed in
The frills on her apron looked like wings

Laced up boots as black as night
A cross round her neck sparkled bright
Elisabeth she said was her name
Then the image broke up as quick as it came

Healing

Healing is love given from the heart
It is accomplished by sending out thoughts
You can send out thoughts for world peace
Smile and help the souls in need

Peace for everything in the universe
The earth, water, animals, fish, and birds
Peace for nuclear armaments and war
For each soldier, killed, lamed, or forlorn

Families, friends, and souls on the streets
Everyone who has lost a loved one and weeps
For all the sick in body and mind
The lame, deaf, dumb, and blind

Hospitals, accidents, stress, our inner fight
Thoughts for ourselves to do what is right
The planet needs healing with your love
What part are you playing, are you doing enough

God

God is not a Spiritualist, Catholic, or Jew
Christian, Moslem, or Hindu
God is the cosmic architect
With perfect laws of cause and effect

The all that is interconnects
With a wisdom beyond our intellect
From the elements, earth, and everything living
God's supreme power permeates everything

This great power is just called love
It can heal the world if used for good,
God's love is here today and tomorrow
Our ultimate challenge is to love another

God Is The Power

God is the power within everything
Life is not possible without this kin
You are part of this universal power
It sustains your spirit every hour

It makes you speak, laugh, and cry
Sense, feel and use your mind
How could you dance, run and walk
See the beauty in one and all

You can see it in the birds and animals
Insects, flowers, fish, and mammal
The wind, rain, stars and suns
We should all keep Gods laws in unison

Add a naught to God, we then have good
Everything good is a facet of love
Love is a power which needs to unfurl
It can bring peace, and healing to the world

Only man doubts Gods spiritual power
Doesn't understand he will live forever
But one fine day man will learn
Everything is spirit on this earth

A Facet Of God

Through the viewfinder a picture unveiled
A carnival procession, with a musical tale
Warm salty air, sand under my feet
Parachutes; pleasure boats, pedal car treats

High cliffs inspire, grassy banks wave
Trees and flowers declare their array
Awakening senses of heavenly smells
Shingle, driftwood, seaweed and shells

Tides cascade foaming white
Sunbeams shimmer with delight
People browse the seaside shops
Gifts, beachwear, and candy floss

Picturesque cottages line the horizon
The hoot of a steam train caused attention
Speed boats dart through white tipped waves
Children, ice cream, buckets and spades

Fishermen hoist full nets on the dock
The marina harbour's luxury yachts
Penny amusements in the arcade
Cars, buses, bikes and trains

Seagulls squawk around the pier
Punch and Judy, create a laugh and tear
A basking shark swam into view
Water skis, inflatable's, the skies blue hue

Al fresco dining along the quay side
Talking, laughing as views blow the mind
Takeaways, cockles, mussels, and pies
Pizzas, curries, fish and fries

Suddenly a band played hymns of praise
An air of reverence fell over the bay
The sunset radiated a golden light
And a facet of God was a wonderful sight

A Rare Seed

Everyone has something to give
Be it words, deeds, or some small gift
But how do you thank a wonderful friend
Only God knows what you have meant

A laugh a chat over tea
Reminiscence and talk of dreams
Words can't express a special bond
You are always there to call upon

Faith and trust are both hidden
No one will know what you have given
My grateful thanks send you love and peace
True friendship is a very rare seed

Birthday

I have no card or envelope
No stamp or letterbox to post
Only paper and pen to write down words
To wish you many Happy Returns

But I can say thank you for been a friend
Past memories and the times we spent
I can wish you good health and peace
Be there to comfort you when in need

I can be a listening ear
Send healing thoughts when your life seems fear
I can hold you in my thoughts to God
And wish for you universal love

∞∞

A String Of Pearls

This string of pearls is only cheap
But they have a meaning you can keep
I do not wish you a pearl of tears
Just pearls of knowledge all your years

If these pearls don't work as said
Trace past footsteps you have tread
Then you will see if you have learnt
The right to give wisdom to the world

Children Of The Earth

Listen children of the earth
You are all part of Gods universe
It doesn't matter what colour you are
Rich, poor, large, or small

Mobile phones, digital sound
Widescreen TVs, computers astound
Wardrobes of shoes, tops, and dresses
Trousers, shirts, makeup, designer glasses

But have you found your gifts in life?
Are you academic or the hands on type?
Material possessions you throw away
Spiritual gifts are for eternity

Have you seen a snowflakes design?
The sun and rain make a rainbow sky
Smelt the perfume of the trees and flowers
Marvelled at natures extraordinary powers

What do you feel in your heart today?
Can you feel love, forgive, and pray
Do you know what is right or wrong?
Are your emotions weak or strong?

One kind word touches someone's soul
What you give comes back three fold
The world is crying for you to fight
Not for materialism, but spiritual light

These are gifts God gives you free
So you have compassion for humanity
So look for your answers deep inside
And let Gods love, be your guiding light

A Facet Of Love

Love is a sensation felt deep inside
It makes you laugh or makes you cry
Without love we would be nothing
No caring, no sharing, no loving

Just like branches on a tree
Love covers many fields
Love for learning something new
The privilege of just been you

The love between husband and wife
They hold the seeds of life
Learning how to give and take
True love cannot separate

The love for a new baby crying
Grief for a loved one dying
The puppy love in adolescence
Love also brings hurtful lessons

Love for our children and families
Relative's friends and different nationalities
The animals, fish, insects, and birds
All the beauty in the world

Love can overcome hate
Heal the suffering, love radiates
Love touches everyone and makes us pause
Because love is an infinite force

A Little Piece Of Heaven

Heaven can be white sands and a turquoise sea
Mountains in mist standing serene
The countryside with magnificent views
Sunlight and its changing hues

Been in a plane watching the sunrise world
Waterfalls and the power they unfurl
Music that stirs the soul inside
Inspirational writers who get in the mind

Cathedrals, Churches, Mosques, and Temples
Stately homes, castles, and architecture
Craftsmen, sculptures, art and design
Stained glass windows which are divine

Plants and flowers which make the world sing
Just been happy with simple things
Rainbows and sunsets that astound
Been on the worlds merry-go-round

Feeling the heartbeat of a City alive
Television, Theatres, the digital vibe
Walking on air when we feel love
Having emotions we learn to trust

Lovely friendships and the animals we love
Family relationships, kisses and hugs
A little piece of heaven to feel and see
Just how wonderful life can be

No Winners

There are no winners in the world
God's laws rule the universe
Life is just an illusion
Emotions add to the confusion

Destiny is pre-determined
Obstacles are part of your learning
They mould the personality
So everything links in society

So why worry about tomorrow
Forgive and forget all your sorrow
Win or lose don't criticise
Because God laws make you wise

Humanity

We have many things to be grateful for
Material things and gods gifts installed
But how do you say thank you for humanity
To friends who trust with simplicity

How do you say thank you for a listening ear
A gentle push when the world is fear
For strength and faith in the unseen
That god exists with a power supreme

How do you thank such wonderful friends?
Life is eternal we can't comprehend
Gifts and money become second reality
Compared to the gift of true humanity

Giving

Let's talk about giving
Not the euro, yen, dollar, or sterling
It's the giving of yourself
Which is the most important wealth?

Do you smile and say hello
To a passer-by or lonely soul
Give your time or a listening ear
Send out healing for those that fear

Can you spare a thought for world peace?
Stand up for what you believe
It doesn't matter what religion you are
Love is the key, not war

∞∞

Mykonos

Windmills turn on top of cliffs
White washed houses covered in mist
Olive trees shade passers by
A deep blue sea meets the sky

Cobbled streets and merchandise
Stunning views before your eyes
A beautiful island that feels unreal
In the middle of nowhere reflecting a dream

Our Thoughts

No one can enter the inner thoughts of the mind
See what we think, and what we hide
It's part of our self, and intimate
So, we have to be aware of what we debate

Thoughts can be impinged upon the mind and heard
They can come from earth, or the spirit world
They can be transmitted for good, or bad
Depends how you think happy or sad

Sometimes mediums go into trance
This takes trust, and meditation
We have to give permission to a spirit being
To control our mind, and what we are saying

We need to be aware of all our thoughts
Use them for good, and not for war
We have our minds for eternity
Remember thought is a living energy

The Gifts Of Christmas

Jesus prophesied Gods wisdom to heal mankind
Today the seeds of his work are still alive
His teachings are taught all over the world
But have they made love and peace unfurl

On Christmas day in Bethlehem
Jesus was born to shed light upon sin
A stable was blessed so legends say
As revelations were revealed that day

Shepherds and peasants from near and far
Were guided to the stable by a star
Kings bestowed gold, frankincense and myrrh
Gifts of love for his birth

A Christmas tradition which never fades
We still exchange gifts bought or made
Packages are wrapped small and large
But have you given from your heart

No matter your circumstances or where you live
Everyone has something special to give
You can send your love in many ways
It doesn't cost a penny, and only a thought away

You can use your energy and your strength
By accepting the work God presents
You can plant your days with positive seeds
By forgiving past hurtful deeds

You can learn something new everyday
So we help ourselves over life's waves
You can open your eyes to nature our mother
See the face of God in all its wonder

You can send your love for universal peace
So negativity can be released
You can send out love to the sick lonely and blind
To the souls who are suffering in body and mind

You can put your faith in the living God
Show an example in the name of love
So let the New Year bells ring anew
So we all look at life, from Gods point of view

Software

Colourful boxes with labels displayed
Fall out of machines day after day
Cardboard, cellophane, manual, CD
Make up the package to be received
Shipped to companies far and wide
Arranged on shelves to catch the eye

Pirate Ship, Toyland, Ready for School
Magic Tales, Cruncher, Maths Blaster 2
Cables, satellites, telephone lines
Keep young imaginations alive
Computers, Monitors, virtual fun
The software world has just begun

The Tree

Magnificent tree you stand out in a crowd
Generations have seen you look proud
You look so stately with branches outstretched
Today dear tree you look your best

You have sheltered everything from the storms
Given birds and insects a home to board
Provided food for insects and animals passing by
Energy, and oxygen, you provide

Now they have come to cut you down
Another supermarket is coming to town
A crunch, creak and then a moan
Crash, bang, a silent overtone

Your golden leaves suddenly take fight
Shining and glistening in the sun light
Twisting and spinning, floating to the ground
Making a carpet of gold and brown

You lay so still in your carpet of gold
Robbed of your heart, but not your soul
All the birds are singing to you
What right has man to be so cruel?

Wood and bracken crunch underfoot
Nuts and acorns are buried in mulch
A new generation will be born again
With new shoots and leaves in the spring

The Mind

Have you ever thought about your mind?
It works in the background like a telephone line
You can't see it, you can't touch
A human computer we learn to trust

The unconscious communicates with the conscious
Through the subconscious mind
With emotions, sensations, and memories we find
The mind is eternal and can never die

The conscious mind is who we are
Our movement, communication, and thought
It can time shift past and present events
An encyclopaedia of knowledge ever present

The minds software is always positive
But virus thoughts become negative
We are all victims of what we think
Because our thoughts are a living thing

Thoughts are recorded good and bad
Onto an eternal subconscious track
Sifted and sorted into files
Negative and positive the mind can't define

The mind can communicate with spheres above
It is all our dreams and our love
It motivates us every day
In everything we do and say

Space stations, the microchip, high speed trains
Are thoughts from the mind, which we claim?
Technology man has achieved
Yet does not recognize his own faculties

We Can't Take A Penny
To The Sphere Above

We can't take a penny to the sphere above
Only our self, our thoughts, and love
So the knowledge we learn on this earth of ours
Will do more good than our sorrows

If earth was a peaceful place
How would we learn, life would be a waste
So walk in daylight, take life as it comes
Then you will see the future in front

Man has a lot to learn, I am afraid
The wars, greed, and problems he creates
There is no need for misery and hate
He will learn one day, if it's not too late

Sun And Moon

Let's think about the sun and moon
Just like peoples life's I presume
There is a dark side and bright side to our life
Do we help ourselves, or do we fight

Moon people build worries one after another
Some seek attention, are suicidal, others don't bother
Others are depressed, lonely, no matter what they do
They all need our help to pull them through

Sun people take another look at life
Try to be positive and slowly strive
They get involved with different things
Join organisations meet other beings

We are all insignificant in the universe
Everyone's life can be reversed
We can help each other when can
By a smile, a chat, and helping hand

It Always Comes To Those That Wait

It always comes to those that wait
There is a right time and a right place
The more we want, we do not get
We get frustrated and upset

We are always where we are meant to be
It's out of our hands, we have to let be
The greater plan has a mission in life
Changes could cause trouble and strife

So if things don't happen in your life
Do not worry and give up the fight
Just be patient and you will find
Everything drops into place at the right time

∞◡∞

Life Is Like A Blackboard

Life is like a blackboard
We can write upon it
Then wipe it clean
By applying positive thinking

What's the good of worrying about life
It only causes illness and strife
All your answers lay within
So except every situation you are in

Dreams

Dreams can be accomplished on the earth
By having an ambition to make them work
You must prove you are worthy first
By overcoming bad times, as lessons learnt

Nothing is impossible there is always a tomorrow
To do your best and forget your sorrow
No one gets more than they can take
It is up to you, the success you make

Without dreams one grows old
There is no future to unfold
So if you want to stay young at heart
Take your dreams by the hand and play your part

Learn to forgive and not resent
Except each situation as heaven sent
What you give you will get back
It could be one of your dreams, remember that

Old Tom

Its only old Tom who wanders around
No one sees him, there's hardly a sound
The house was Toms before he died
Now new people are changing the inside
Workmen are walking in and out
Knocking down walls and causing a fright
They are changing all the cupboard doors
Running electric cable, and pipes under the floor
In goes a new boiler, and lots of plugs
Tom is devastated he dare not look

Tom doesn't believe in the after life
He could be happy with his wife
Tom needs to go to his life above
Doesn't realise that he is loved
He will stay on the earth wandering around
Until his thoughts change his mind
We can help Tom understand
He needn't be lonely, as help is at hand
We can help his family to unite
By sending him love to go to the light

Seek And Find

Listen children seek and find
All about your psychic mind
You are the future mediums
To prove that life continues

Your world is full of technology
But man hasn't researched his own faculties
The spirit world can help you discover
There are endless fields to uncover

The bible quotes test ye the spirits
By their fruits they shall be known
All you need is faith, and trust in god
Make sure what you do, you do it with love

∽∾

Spiritual Eyes

Look at life with spiritual eyes
See the water, earth, and skies
Feel fresh air upon your face
Creation is the wonder of every race
The pulse of life beats out and sings
God's love and power is in everything

We Are All Actors

We are all actors on the stage
Each playing a part in the human race
Good and bad have a part to play
So we learn something new everyday

It could be sadness, illness, or loss
Happiness or general stuff
We have different emotions for different parts
No one can see what's in our heart

Our lines are compassion, peace and love
Takes endless practice and rehearsals
So what great mind created this play?
God of cause, so we strive for eternity

ംു

Listen And Advise

Listen and advise, then clear it from your mind
You are not been selfish you are been wise
Give of yourself in time and caring
A problem is halved just by sharing

If you take others problems onto yourself
It will deplete your energy, then you will need help
A clear mind helps everyone more
You will be able to deal with the problem in store

You Are Never Too Old

You are never too old to take a degree
I knew a man who was eighty three
Who wanted to prove he was intelligent
But waited years to get the chance

Born into a family of poverty
There was no hope of going to university
He was sent down the mines at fourteen
To earn a shilling for his keep

The war broke out he went to fight
Then followed the general strike
He married and had a family
Worked shifts at the local factory

No his dream had not backfired
There was time to study when he retired
Three degrees took five years of studying
The letters after his name don't mean a thing

This man had faith, faith in himself
Old but happy he has achieved his wealth
So if you have an ambition makes it come true
Have faith in yourself and the potential within you

Love

Love is a cosmic force
The creator's supreme law
Perfection rules its origin
Without love we are nothing

Love moulds the soul's personality
Its mission is to serve humanity
The creed is peace in the universe
Love asks for nothing in return

Love can be ecstatic or pain
The laugh of sunshine, or tears of rain
It is giving and receiving
Love radiates light on understanding

Love forgives and forgets trivialities
It is simplicity, hope, and charity
Graced with ultimate faith
Any obstacle love can face

Love is beyond any language
It never takes advantage
Love permeates every living thing
We live and move within its being

Love is sensed by an emotion deep inside
Which ebbs and flows like the tide?
A total experience no one can fight
Because love is the essence of life

Not For Sale

We can't buy love
Emotions, or trust
The stars, moon, and sun
Nor the planets in unison
Thunder, lighting, fire or a tornado
Sunlight, darkness and a rainbow

We can't buy nature, wind, rain or snow
Trees, flowers, and everything that grows
We can't buy the essence that makes you and me
The animals, insects, fish and sea
We can't buy happiness, laughter, or today
None can be purchased, sold, or given way

Heaven And Hell

You can't see heaven
You can't see hell
They are states of mind
Within yourself

You are as you think
You plant the seeds
Happy or sad
What yield do you reap?

You can't go back
You can't go forward
Here and now you are free
You decide your path and needs

Stress

Would you worry in a hundred years' time?
Stress is a killer when it gets in the mind
You need to be positive every day
Hard I know, but the only way

By keeping on an even keel
Vibrations form a water-wheel
They flow into streams, rivers, and sea
Which holds everything you need

So take from the sea what you want
But remember waves, will miss the point
When you except things as they are
You will open a brand new door

Life's lessons make us wise
They allow our inner spirit to strive
Our time on earth is a flash in the pan
So we must do the best we can

The Stone

What's it like to be a stone
Have no feelings, or emotion
Take, take, take, from everything you do
Be so selfish, be so cruel

What's it like to be buried in snow
Thinking of self and no other soul
Surly the rain can thaw you out
To take another look at life

What's it like when the sun shines
Doesn't it touch your conscious mind?
Not to be kind, helpful, and give
Without love, how can anyone live

Freedom

I will never understand
Man's inhumanity to man
We all have to learn good and bad
Now it seems the world has gone mad

We all think that we are free
But no one understands what it means
Nearly everyone lives in fear as I speak
With bombs, knives, drugs, and guns on the streets

We need to stand up for freedom and peace
Stop the wars, rape, hatred, and prejudices
Talk to each other and compromise
There's more good in the world than we realize

What's happened to kindness in our hearts?
Chosen leaders must play their part
Have compassion, and see what's wrong
Make changes, so everyone can sing a peaceful song

It's Raining

The sun shines through a rainy day
People are walking through puddles and spray
Buses, umbrellas, cars and Macs
Trainers, hoods and anoraks

Every tree, flower and plant
Are bathed in rain drops giving thanks
A giant rainbow embraces the sky
Nature's glory sends energies high

Every colour is beamed down
Healing people as they travel around
Smiles and waves from a rickshaw
Love and hugs from buses and cars

So why are we living in a world so torn
Of greed, destruction, poverty and war
We must change and learn to share
With patience, and tolerance we need to care

Nearly every country is mixed race
Different religions and cultures to embrace
Everyone has a right to be here
Our responsibility is to love, not fear

Lonely Sea

O lonely sea
Tossing and turning like my sleep
Am I living, or is this a dream
Waves crash and foam over rocks
Waiting, waiting for the sun to come up

O vast ocean
I can't see your horizon
Reflections create misty skies
How cruel you look turning tides
Waiting, waiting for the sun to rise

O full moon
Shimmering silver in eerie gloom
Casting shadows over sand dunes
Creating a city before my eyes
Waiting, waiting for the sun to shine

O lonely sea
We both have an affinity
There is life beneath you and life in me
How warm we both can become
Waiting, waiting for the sun

Problems

Everyone has problems, trouble and strife
How would we learn about our life
They are gifts that create our personality
So we have to experience things in reality

If you can't see daylight yourself
You can ask for additional help
Just ask a loved one in the spirit world
If they can help you to unfurl

The answer will not be given right away
But put in your thoughts another day
Your problems will be shown in a different light
So you will be able to put things right

I must stress we have a path to take
Answers come for our own sake
Our loved ones know what is best
Please give them thanks, and say god bless

The Crystal

What can I give you from the heart
For been in my life when things were dark
A listening ear, a visit a chat
Built my confidence so I could laugh

I can't give flowers they don't last
Jewellery is a personnel task
But a beautiful crystal filled with love
Hangs in a window so you can look

A crystal is charged by the sun
Its energy is infinite and unison
Loving rainbows are sent everyday
No matter what plight comes your way

The World

The world is a catastrophe
Violent and full of greed
Inflation soars everywhere
Pollution slowly fills the air

Third world communities starve and die
Fighting and looting all rate high
Shops and factories just close down
Unemployment in every town

Prejudice with different races
Men strike for higher wages
Government disputes miss the core
Nuclear armaments are built for war

What future do the children face?
Qualifications will be a waste
Under currents fill the air
Thieves, drugs, does anyone care,

Man is cutting down the trees
Global warming will end the freeze
Food waste, and rubbish is not desired
Earthquakes, tornado's floods, and fires

Bombs explode in buses and trains
Buried land mines kill and lame
Aids, cancer, and heart disease
Animal rights campaign the streets

Shipyards and mines are monuments
Homeless people carry cardboard tents
Computer technology leads the way
Hackers break codes for money each day

This was not the universal plan
We should learn to understand
Our life is only for a short time
What a legacy to leave behind-

We Are Human Beings

We are human beings at the end of the day
It's part of life what we do and say
Sometimes we say things we don't mean
It's a natural reaction to problems unseen

Its armour to protect what we believe
But it causes chaos, breakups, and disbelief
Makes one retaliate, resentful, and mistrust
But life is too short to hold a grudge

Problems teach lessons of a different kind
Self-control, tolerance, and peace of mind
We must learn to forgive and not resent
Not look back and look to the present

We can't judge what other people do
Cause and effect will sort out the truth
To forgive with love in your heart
Will make you wise to play life's part

Pride

If your fight is pride
Let god decide
You can't judge another person's life
Their conscious mind has to decide

Everyone is given a second chance
To change their own circumstance
Meet difficult situations half way through
You will half the problem you could not do

The spirit must learn from good and bad
From every experience happy or sad
No one is wrong no one is right
So how can pride be a fight?

∞∞

Take A Risk

Don't be afraid to take a risk
Opportunities are not to be missed
Use your intuition to see if it feels right
As we can't see the picture of life

You may be apprehensive and not bother
But every experience leads to another
Life is short we have no time to wait
Succeed or fail, we learn and create

Marriage

Marriage is a partnership
Blessed with love it becomes a ship
Sailing over the rough and smooth
Giving and taking is its fuel

Every experience is cause and effect
No one is perfect, so give each respect
Harsh words are not forgotten
Breed resentments which get hidden

Both take the helm on an even keel
But don't be afraid to express how you feel
Life's storms and waves crash unseen
So always live within your means

Share each other's interests with enthusiasm
And remember to show your appreciation
Keep your minds active with dreams
So tides ebb and flow into scenes

Never forget you are children of God
Embark on Gods course which radiates love
Then when you look back at your happiness and strife
You will see Gods lighthouse has navigated your life

Wealth

Let's talk about giving
Not the euro, yen, dollar, or sterling
It's the giving of yourself
Which is the most important wealth?

A wealth that cannot be bought
Destroyed or taught
Because it is earned
By your life and thoughts

You take this wealth to the spirit world
Its far more important than the wealth on earth
The scales must balance evenly
Both spiritually and materially

Do you smile and say hello
To a passer-by or lonely soul
Give your time or a listening ear
Send out healing far and near

Are you sending thoughts for world peace?
Do you stand up for what you believe?
It doesn't matter what religion you are
Love is the wealth which will open the door

Worry

Would you worry in one hundred years' time?
Stress is a killer when it gets in the mind
If you try to think positive every day
Everything will fall into place

How can you say that, you are not in my place?
Because positivity is an energy to embrace
As you think so you are
Emanations spread wide and far

By accepting things the way they are
You will open a brand new door
Life is lessons everyday
But it is up to ourselves the success we make

Lessons in life make one wise
We are allowing our inner spirit to strive
Our time on earth is a flash in the pan
So we must learn as much as we can

Crossroads

Are you at a cross road in your life?
Confused not knowing which way to strive
Frustration lays deep within
Because you want to do the right thing

Times like these come to trial
So, look at life with a smile
You need to make changes with your life
It could be material or spiritual light

It may be a job, or a move
You may need spiritual food
Learn to say no, or learn something new
Express another part of you

There is always a door with keys in the lock
You can open the door, or keep it shut
But if you risk going through the door
A whole new life will be in store

Responsibility

We are all responsible for our self
Try to except your life and what it presents
There is a time to laugh a time to cry
This is written in your book of life

When you feel lonely and hard up
It is given so we appreciate the good
Except it as a lesson you need to face
At times we all need time to recuperate

You have your changes in your hands
What you think will expand
Your thoughts are a living energy
So, put them to good use everyday

The Lamp Factory

I worked in a lamp factory
As a lamp assembler in a pottery
Monday to Friday I clocked in come what may
There was only eight hours to pass away

My bench is full of hundreds of pots
I felt like smashing the whole darned lot
I drill the pots, and base sides
Then nuts and washers I have to find

I saw the rods, and assemble the pots
Remembering to screw a lamp holder on top
Then I wired up the lamps, put sand in the top
Stacked them on pallets, bound for posh shops

Every day was the same
Sometimes I wondered if I was insane
Super work colleagues made my day
I had a job, got paid, and had a laugh everyday

Zombies

Everyone would be zombies lost in time
If we didn't have a mind
Can you imagine what life would be
No one would have any individuality

All our memories happy and sad
Are recorded on an eternal track
This complex piece of machinery
Works in the background with simplicity

Any section of your life
Can be recalled day or night
The mind will always be free
Because there is nothing to touch and nothing to see

Moving House

We are moving house again
Fourth time lucky, back to Devon
The Lorries arrived, furniture is stacked
Everything is loaded and well packed

One last look around the house
It's so empty there's not a sound
When we moved in the house was a shell
We gave it our love, and it served us well

Mixed emotions begin to hover
What will a new house be like I wonder?
New surroundings are waiting for us
Lots of work ahead I trust

It could be good it could be bad
But right now I feel sad
Leaving familiar faces behind
To begin again a brand new life

Holland

There is no work in our town
All the factories are on short time
You have to contract overseas
In Holland where I can't be

How lonely and sad you must feel
All alone in a strange country
No one you know, no family to see
Even a different language to speak

Just hope we don't grow apart
I trust you with all my heart
Your love for me, my love for you
Is strong enough to see us through

Come rain come shine, come what may
My love is with you everyday
I would be with you if I could
We have children stay here I must

Over The Air

Over the air your flight is called
We have only minutes left
You pick up your bags, we walk to the gate
Words unspoken goodbyes I hate

Tears in our eyes trying not to show
Behind dark glasses faces of woe
A look, a hug, a kiss
No one will know how much you are missed

Up into the blue sky roars the plane
Taking you my love away again
Please keep him safe to God I pray
As I got a glimpse of your final wave

I watch the plane in the sunlight
Getting smaller and smaller out of sight
So listen husband flying in the clouds
Remember your wife here on the ground

You left me memories to hold awhile
Your face, emotion, your last smile
You said you loved me and I was your life
I guess I can face those lonely nights

You Are Never Alone

You are never alone, no matter where you are
My thoughts can be sent from afar
There is a wonderful link between us both
We know how each feels, before words are spoke

Your never alone I can feel
I can hold you close as tight as can be
Can you feel my arms around your body?
When your alone and have nobody

I am with you every day
Lighting your path come what may
By holding on and being strong
We can create a feeling that we belong

To Have You Here

To have you here , what I would give
It seems that we are going adrift
Theses lonely days, and lonely nights
Without you here, life is a fight

To feel your kiss, just once more
Your arms around me to feel secure
I need you here with me again
Be together but that's in vain

How much longer can we be strong
Your contract in Holland, goes on and on
When you're not here I don't want to live
To have you here, what I would give

Welcome Home

Welcome home my love welcome back
Four years of contracts end at last
As the minutes tick away
I just wait impatiently
For you to walk through the door
To hug and hold you close once more

I am so excited can it be real
These crazy feelings that I feel
Can't you hear my heart beating
I can't wait for our meeting
Is this reality at long last
Welcome home my love welcome back

Poems created 1986

My Daughters

Two daughters god loaned me
To love, teach then set free
One is dark the other fair
Between them both I can't compare

Both are beautiful in my eyes
With lovely faces, eyes and smiles
Each one is clever in their field
What a proud mother I have been

One is quiet the other outgoing
Two little ladies now are growing
Both have a special place in my heart
When they leave home, it will tear me apart

∞∞∞

Children

Children are loaned to us by God
You can only love them, guide them, teach them
Then let them go
Remember that they have lessons and a life to lead
Just the same as you and me.

A Mothers Love

Daughters you part of God and part of me
Never under estimate how a mother feels
Because lots of love always comes your way
To take away the rain, when your life is grey

It flies to you on the wings of love
You can't see it, you can't touch
Pure and gentle yet so free
Surrounds you in peace and security

If my love puts a smile upon your face
Clears your mind when it's in a maze
Gives you patents and self-control
To obey the prompting of your soul

Helps you forgive and not resent
Look to yourself for criticisms
Makes you strong to do your best
Think about the law of cause and effect

Let you put others before your self
Pray for the souls who need help
Respect every colour, cast, and creed
Be kind to every creature's needs

If it lets you find peace within
Then walk with God in everything
Because the origin of love comes from god
If my love touches you, I have fulfilled my job

Forever a Mother

My Mum

Mum you are the sunshine and the rain
Yet so distant like the prairie plane
What would I do without you their
To share my life with all its cares
I know you love the everyday things
The happiness and sorrows my life brings
You know it all like a book
Page after page who else could look

Only a mother who bore a child
And gave it a special love when it cried
Taught it good manners and how to be strong
Showed the difference between right and wrong
Gave it faith in God above
To do their duty in life with love
Let them strive on their own two feet
To learn the lessons the spirit needs.

No other mother could take your place
How could I help the human race?
Lift a lost soul to seek spiritual light
Give them faith in the after life
Teach them to rise above earthy things
To show them that god is in everything
Only a mother special and rare
Could give me life, and the wisdom to care

Thank You Dear Father

Thank you dear father
For looking after me
Making me stand on my own two feet
You taught me good manners, and how to dance
Play darts, cards, fish, and take a chance

Thank you dear father
For all your sayings poems, songs and stories
That live in my heart in all their glory
You were a showman with genuine charm
Who had everyone captivated in your palm

Thank you dear father
For the wisdom and love you bestowed
Making everyone laugh when times were hard
A wonderful father and grandfather too
Everyone loves, and misses you

Poem created 1997

The Spirit Of The Universe

I AM THE ALL THAT IS SAYS THE UNIVERSE

I am everything that exists, and that has existed, and
everything that will exist
My contents include space, solar systems, planets, moons,
stars, suns, and galaxies
We all have a connection with God the Spirit and Power
of the universe, the all that is
Yet do we recognise the opportunities that come as
spiritual tests.
Do we look inside our self, look at our conscious, and our
motives?
Do you do what is right and just for your Solar system
housing planet earth?
You are responsible for your planet and everything living
on it
If you don't look after your planet, cause and effect will
come into operation, action and reaction.

I AM BEAUTIFUL, I AM MAGNIFICENT

HEY LOOK AT ME SAYS PLANET EARTH

I am a beautiful planet I provide the land for you to walk
upon and build upon.
I make your mountains, rocks, sea, rivers, forests and
national parks.
You plant your seeds in me so you can grow food and
plants.
I support your trees and flowers; I support you, and all
creatures great and small
In fact I support all life.
I work with nature like a huge machine as long as I am
not polluted
But humans blow me up, plant rubbish, and nuclear
waste inside me.
You spray poisons, pesticides, and all sorts of toxic
chemicals to choking me.
So I retaliate with other elements to create earthquakes,
volcanoes, and tsunamis, which can destroy far more than
you can in seconds.
Just remember that you do not need atomic bombs to
destroy your planet, together with all the other elements
working together we can destroy far more than you can
imagine in minutes

YOU CAN'T DO WITHOUT ME I AM PART OF GOD

DON'T FORGET ME SAYS WIND

My wind energy is clean as I do not pollute your air
I disperse all your seeds from plants all over the world
My power can make electricity from wind turbines and
waves
I can move moisture from your weather, land, and
deserts, and cool your planet
I am the breeze on a hot day, the typhoon, and my
hurricanes and dust storms can be deadly destroying
everything in my path.

YOU CAN'T DO WITHOUT ME I AM PART OF GOD

LISTEN TO ME SAYS THE SOLAR SYSTEM

I am part of the universe and have many solar systems
which consists of the sun as a central star, the moon,
planets which include earth, all revolve round me
I also house objects like asteroids comets and meteoroids
Planet earth is polluting me with space junk, a space
station, rockets are sent from earth, and nuclear bombs
destroy parts of me, crashed space craft junk floats about,
and hundreds of defunct satellites are now cluttering my
premises.
Thousands of planes come into my atmosphere polluting
me, and earth is destroying my ozone layers which in turn
creates global warming.
I need to be cleaned up and fast

YOU CAN'T DO WITHOUT ME I AM PART OF GOD

OK SAYS TREE

You forget I am part of the universe too, majestic and a
powerful healer
I prevent your soil from erosion, and help water
pollution,
I provide security and homes for insects, birds, bees, and
animals.
I provide food and berries to eat.
I prevent floods but you cut me down to make more land,
paper, and wood,
You forget I absorb the carbon dioxide, and create the
oxygen you breathe, and clean your air of pollution.
I am part of global warming too

YOU CAN'T DO WITHOUT ME I AM PART OF GOD

WHAT ABOUT US SAID THE HUMBLE FLOWERS

We are the earth's rainbow expressing god's love and
healing.
We grow in all kinds of conditions to show you that
beauty is everywhere.
The herbs we produce are the earth's medicine.
We send out perfume with exotic smells.
We work with wind to spread pollen to the same flower
We produce seeds found in fruit,
Bees take our nectar to make honey
Some flowers you eat, such as seeds, petals, vegetables,
and spices

WE ARE ALSO PART OF GOD

NOW LOOK AT ME SAID THE SUN

I give off light and warm your atmosphere else it would
be rocks ice and darkness.
I provide vitamin D and strength for you to have energy.
Everything needs light to survive and grow.
I am your beautiful sunrises and sunsets
Without me you would starve as the plants use my light to
create food, and oxygen for everything to breathe
My light through solar power is turned into electricity.
My ultraviolet light can kill bacteria and other organisms
in the air and in your water.
I also work with the moon reflecting light at night
My light is part of the life force I am magnificent.

YOU CAN'T DO WITHOUT ME I AM PART OF GOD

LISTEN TO ME SAID FIRE

My fire is the most dangerous element in the world
I am so hard to contain when out of control
You can't touch me as I am very hot and burn
So can leave horrific injuries and death
My fire can destroy cities, forests, land, houses, and
everything in its path
No one should mess with my fire
I can be useful when used properly for fuel

YOU CANT DO WITHOUT ME I AM PART OF GOD

NOW LISTEN TO ME SAYS THE MOON

You forget that I control your tides
I am a satellite and orbit the earth and stabilize the earth's
rotation
I dictate the seasons and the length of your days
I transmit light of the back of the sun which enables you
to see at night
I may look dark but I am the light at the end of the tunnel
when things get bad
I give everything time to rest, reflect, and experience.
There is no perfection with me. Everything needs the
darkness to grow
I AM PART OF GOD

NOW TAKE NOTE, SAID RAIN,

Listen said the rain I am your fresh drinking water I fill
your ponds, rivers, streams, lakes, sea and oceans. I am the
snow, the perfect snowflake, ice, and rainbow.
Everything would die without my water.
We are not drenched enough, and together with acid rain
rivers and lakes are becoming poison.
I am also your electric thunder storms; my thunder is
caused by lightening though the sudden increase in
pressure and temperature, when cold air overlaps damp
warm air.
Lightening is an electrical discharge and my bolts carry
thousands of amps of electric current which can kill
humans, and can destroy houses if not grounded, my
lightening also creates fires, tornadoes, and hurricanes

I AM A LIVING ENERGY

LISTEN TO US SAID SEA AND OCEAN

We affect the whole planet.
I am partially enclosed by land and smaller than the deep
waters of the ocean said sea
We hold nearly all of the planets salt water; we produce
more than half your oxygen, and absorb carbon from it.
We support all kinds of marine life from the fish, salt,
seaweed, and other food you eat. We are a home to
beautiful corals reefs, sea grasses and all sorts of different
plants and species.
Our waves make electricity and power generators,
Ships and all kinds of boats use us travel
We get blown up, not drenched enough, all kinds of
plastic, sewage, nets, fishing lines, oil, toxins, and all sorts
of rubbish is dumped inside us.
Sea and river creatures are eating poison, and some
species are not growing properly
Hugh tankers leak oil destroying beautiful coasts and wild
life.
You create acid rain, and we try hard to remove the earth's
toxics
We all have violent tempers and get very angry with
thunder and lightening
You forget we can interact with the sun, wind, and
ourselves to create floods, storms, hurricanes, freezing
temperatures, tsunamis, and can wipe out huge cities in
minutes.

YOU CAN'T DO WITHOUT US WE ARE PART OF GOD

I HAVE LISTENED TO YOU ALL SAID ATMOSPHERE

You all go on at how wonderful you are but I am the
breath of life, everything living relies on me for life and
growth.
My atmosphere shields nearly everything from the suns
radiation
I used to have the correct atmosphere and temperature to
support everything on the earth now my atmosphere is
polluted
I contain all the gases that air needs so everything can
breathe, and I protect everything from the heat and
radiation of the sun.
I warm your planet by day and I cool it at night
Now due to human foolishness you have created global
warming which is melting the ice, and creating the
greenhouse effect, stop polluting me, my atmosphere is
been poisoned
I am very worried as everything living relies on me for life
and growth.

YOU CAN'T DO WITHOUT ME I AM PART OF GOD

Poems created 2009

John Philip Driscoll

Always a welcome always a smile
This was mainly my husband's style
Sit down, I'll make tea
Then we can discuss your shopping spree

Forty years of memories are always there
Can never be taken away, only shared
We talked, and talked with laughs and tears
Shared ups and downs and good years

John gave me the freedom to express
But teased me to bits, none the less
He gave me faith in myself
And opened my eyes to life itself

I really miss those laughing eyes
His mischievous look when he had a surprise
A husband in a million is hard to find
God bless you John, I will see you in time

My Brave Husband

You were a vibrant action man
Full of surprises nine times out of ten
To love someone and share everything
Be it good or bad, is a life worth living

We had three days then we would part
Felt like someone had stabbed my heart
Shock, anguish, pain, and tears
You were so brave to face your fears

We carried on and nothing was said
You didn't moan, or get upset
You just excepted it was your time
Your courage and bravery was divine

I had to let you pass in peace
Knowing one day we would meet
My thoughts and love are sent everyday
Thank you for been my husband, friend, and stay

A Passing

A large black cloud hangs in the air
We both have feelings of despair
No time to talk we only have hours
Before the rain comes and drowns our sorrows

Suddenly we are lifted onto a peaceful sphere
I held your hand as you passed without fear
A wonderful peace filled the room
I know you will come back to me very soon

Now it's raining hard outside
How can I live now you have died
Clouds of emotion keep passing me by
I hope one day the sun will shine

A Mountain

A passing is like climbing the highest mountain
On the other side love flows like a fountain
Mountains divide each one of us
But we all meet again in god's love

How Can I Live?

How can I live all alone?
Is this the fairy-tale zone?
You're not here anymore
To walk again through the door

Left with photos to see your smile
Videos bring realism for a while
Part of my heart has gone missing
No more hugs, no more kissing

We had happiness and strive
This was all part of our life
But what about all our dreams
On the back burner, it's so unreal

They say it gets better over time
But now I have a mountain to climb
You have proved life after death
But I miss you; miss you, with every breath

Miss You, Miss You

Miss you, miss you, yes indeed
How I wish you were here with me
Your look, your kiss, our endless speech
Our laughter and your gentle squeeze

Now you have passed its hard to survive
You were the light of my life
But in my sadness I am glad
To have our memories happy and sad

How cruel of life to turn the tide
Just when we had both retired
Miss you, miss you, yes indeed
How I wish you were here with me

The Merry Go Round

Life has only just turned round
To enjoy a retirement merry go round
So why have you died we had plans
Everything's been taken out of our hands

I miss your presence every day
The jokes, banter, music, and play
It hurts so much it feels unfair
With only the spirit world to share

You have put thoughts inside my head
To help me through the days ahead
My love is with you everywhere
Till we meet again please take care

Silence

We talked and talked
Now there is silence
We laughed and laughed
Now there is silence
We joked and joked
Now there is silence

We had ups and downs
Now there is silence
We sang and sang
Now there is silence
We danced and danced
Now there is silence

We listened and listened
Now there is silence
We kissed and hugged
Now there is silence
We are now mind to mind
In total silence

Our House

Our house feels empty and full of gloom
Your aura has gone from every room
The happy atmosphere has gone
Only our memories linger on

My emotions have been torn apart
Nothing left but a broken heart
There is no interest any more
I just sit staring at the wall

Feels like time has stood still for a while
But I must be brave and put on a smile
You were my husband good friend too
My whole life I shared with you

When we were together we were a team
The things we did made our dream
I know we will meet again one day
May god be with you every day

We Miss You

We miss you; miss you why have you died
Everyone has feelings, and we have all cried
Yet love has been sent to you everyday
To heal your spirits, and light your way

It's the little things we all love to share
We miss you lots and really care
Surly you can feel our thoughts
You touched our lives, now we are apart

Life is just an endless book
Which we open, read. Or close shut
Negative, positive, advance or retire
New chapters begin when we desire

They say time heals a broken heart
Don't let a passing rip life apart
Pease please let the sun shine through
We all meet again, and then we will join you

Mirrors

Different mirrors in my mind
Reflect our memories one at a time
Tears have fallen like pouring rain
Will we be strangers, when we meet again

All the things that we have shared
Our love and how we cared
We always let each other be free
Yet we were one to each other's needs

Now we are both in different worlds
Struggling, struggling, to unfurl
You have your life , I have mine
Yet we are together in thought and mind

So goodbye my love, please take care
Just remember your wife, who can't be there
Our tears of joy, our tears of pain
Our tears of happiness when we meet again

Do You Love Me

Do you love me, can it be true
I am so scared of losing you
You say you love me, and you care
Only me your life to share

Yet here alone I sit in vain
Even love doesn't feel the same
When we are together we are strong
Everyone knows we are one

I wonder what you are thinking
I only hope our minds are linking
Do you love me can it be true
Can't you see, I love you

❧

Different Worlds

We are in different worlds you and I
Yet we can still laugh, talk, and cry
I can help you, and you can help me
Like new branches growing on a tree
Visions of reality, will be the seeds
Firmly grown, when we meet

Is This Love

Is this love I have felt
Only god can answer
Even love don't feel the same
When you're not here to ease the pain

Anguish and doubt come to mind
Waves of tears fill my eyes
Emptiness lies deep inside
The gap between us seems so wide

I miss your hugs, kiss and chats
Even your hot temper created laughs
All our music and memories lay
In our hearts and minds today

Do you feel the same as me
You are smiling now, I can see
Is this love that I have felt?
Only god can answer

Heaven Sent

I wondered if you were heaven sent
Then God sent us a box of presents
Containing ups, downs, tears, and joy
So many lessons we had to employ

This was hard for us both
We needed to learn how to cope
Without love, give and take
There would have been lots of mistakes

We learnt to respect each other's views
Gave each other freedom for hobbies anew
Shared loss, chores, illness and strife
Coped with separations to modernise a house

We put our trust in the unseen
So we could hopefully open a dream
Friendships, holidays, and priceless things
Every box we opened we learnt something

Then the penny dropped when I opened a box
God gave us present I had not thought of
We had experienced every present together
Because we were heaven sent to each other

My Wonderful Husband John

The handle went on the bedroom door
As it opened I looked in awe
Happy Christmas love, I heard you say
Standing as solid as me in the doorway

The smile on your face was full of mischief
Same laughing eyes, it was beyond belief
You had more hair, your pod had gone
No lines on your face, you looked handsome

Your check shirt looked like new
Same casual trousers, just like you
Your face and arms were slightly tanned
Then you closed the door, as I finished the scan

I knew you would come back to me
But even I didn't expect this treat
It was 6.00am on Christmas day
What better present can a loved one convey

John passed 28th April 2009
This happened Christmas day 2009

Live, Live, Live

When you lose someone you love
It's hard to start a new life and trust
Seems like a dream, and you want to retreat
But you have a life you need to complete

Make a bucket list, and then follow it through
Could be hobbies, holidays, and things anew
We could take a course, or volunteer
Meeting new people is not to fear

By having coffee and a chat with a friend
Breaks up the day, so loneliness ends
We all have potential, and god's gifts
Try to find you again, and live, live, live

Without You

Without you here, I am not living
Part of me is missing
Everything seems unreal
Just like living in a dream

Lots of things are going on
But I am just floating along
I can't believe you have passed
Time will heal, our friendship will last

I gave you my heart
But now we are apart
I have to sort things out without you
Build a new life, to see me through

I know I must be very strong
Not hold you back that would be wrong
Our love will get us both though
Till once again I meet you

My Life

Throughout most of my life
I have experienced trouble and strife
But I have got good reason to smile
I am not bitter I am wise

God shared everything with me
I was taught lessons to help humanity
Angels were sent to keep me strong
Courage was given to carry on

God just excepted me the way I am
It did not matter if I was right or wrong
God's love never changes and does not judge
Because love is the essence of everything good